Gucci Mane Book - A Biography of Greatness:

The Life and Times of Gucci Mane Legendary Hip-Hop Trap Rapper

By JJ Vance

Table of Contents

Disclaimer and Note to Readers:

This is an unofficial tribute book to Gucci Mane from a fan, for a fan to support his legacy.

The information in this book has been provided for educational and entertainment purposes only.

The information contained in this book has been compiled from sources deemed reliable and it is accurate to the best of the Author's knowledge; however, the Author cannot guarantee its accuracy and validity and cannot be held liable for any errors or omissions.

The fact that an individual or organization is referred to in this document as a citation or source of information does not imply that the author or publisher endorses the information that the individual or organization provided. This is an unofficial fan tribute book and has not been approved or endorsed by the Gucci Mane or his associates.

Download Your Free Gift!

Thanks for checking out **"Gucci Mane Book - A Biography of Greatness: The Life and Times of Gucci Mane Legendary Hip-Hop Trap Rapper"** – You have made a wise choice in picking up this book!

Because you're about to discover many interesting tidbits of Gucci Mane you've never knew before!

But before you go any further, I'd like to offer you a free gift.

My Ultimate Collection of Links to Gucci Mane's YouTube Videos!

If you're a Gucci Mane fan, you'll DROOL over this!

<u>But I'll take it down if too many people claim it as it's my personal treasure</u>. *Don't miss out!*

Get it before it expires here:

https://bit.ly/GucciManeBonus

Or Scan the QR Code:

GUCCI MANE: INTRODUCTION

Ups and downs, high and low points. Wash. Rinse. Repeat.

No other words capture the evolution of Radric Davis as perfectly as the last paragraph of his 2017 *New York Times* bestselling memoir, *The Autobiography of Gucci Mane*, and so we will start with them:

I've taken heed of that. To start a new chapter you've got to turn the page on the last one. Still every now and then I do think it's okay to stop and look back, just for a moment, before continuing on your way. Especially when it's a hell of a story.

And it *is* one hell of a story.

From a repeat offender with several run-ins with the law to a 2020 collaboration with Italian fashion powerhouse Gucci, only a handful of public figures in the 21st century can boast to having a career as prolifically dynamic and culturally relevant as the American rapper. Among many other things, he has been cited on several occasions for his groundbreaking contributions to the subgenre of hip hop known as trap music.

Nowadays, it seems far-fetched that the hip-hop/R&B legend eked out a living by selling crack cocaine in East Atlanta's suburbs at one point in time. Sometimes going out in the pouring rain to carry out his trade while blowing into his hands to retain a fraction of body warmth.

In this book, we will be taking an extensive look into the course of Gucci Mane's life story, from his humble beginnings in Bessemer, Alabama, to his meteoric rise to stardom and the infamy while going back decades and looking into his music career, which spans two decades.

By the time we draw this book to a close, everything will be brought under the spotlight, including the controversies and his impact on pop culture today. It will be obvious that as long as you're determined and you set your mind to it, achieving success while living your best life is not a dream but very much a possibility.

In many ways, this is a story of nature versus nurture; being on the come up and losing your way. At the same time, it is one of hope, and perhaps most importantly, entirely based on real events.

But you already know this.

GUCCI MANE: THE BEGINNING

BESSEMER

His parents met in 1978. Two years later, on the 12th of February 1980, Radric Delantic Davis would be born in Bessemer, a southwestern suburb of Birmingham, Alabama.

At the time of his birth, his father, Ralph Everett Dudley, had been in Detroit, Michigan, running from the authorities on drug charges. This is why he was not around to sign the birth certificate, explaining why he took his mother's last name. Like himself, he has said his first name Radric was a product of his parent's union: half Ralph, half Vicky.

There is a history of enlistment into military service in his family.

James Dudley Sr., who was Radric's father's father, i.e., his paternal grandfather (born April 15, 1920), was in service in the military for twelve years as a cook and fought in World War II. After which, he went on to teach radio and television before later working as a postman. Walter Lee Davis, his mother's father, was also in service, as a cook, on the USS *South Dakota*. However, he fought in the October 1942 Battle of Santa Cruz, where he was grievously injured. Upon his move to Bessemer, he would find work as one of the first Black supervisors in a meat packaging company. His father enlisted in the U.S. Army in 1973 after graduating from high school. He was stationed in South Korea for two years.

Gucci Mane cites his father as the source of his stage name and explains that Ralph fell in love with the Gucci brand during the time he spent in Italy in the service. An older cousin of his began to call him the "Gucci man."

The *Mane,* he says, comes from a Southern twist on *man.*

Before she met Ralph, his mother, Vicky Jean Davis, had a son, Victor, from a previous relationship. She was a social worker and a teacher. Because she was pursuing her college degree, he was raised by his paternal grandmother, Olivia Dudley, one of the people mentioned in his autobiography's dedication. The second is his grandfather, Walter Davis Sr., with who he was also very close.

Walter died of a heart attack in front of him. Gucci Mane has said that his passing marked the beginning of the end of his living in Bessemer.

Gucci Mane attended Jonesboro Elementary. By the time he enrolled in kindergarten, he was more advanced than his peers since his mother taught him to read when he was very young. In Sunday school, his teachers were always surprised that he could read and recite scripture from the Bible.

Gucci Mane stated in a 2019 YouTube interview with radio presenter Charlamagne Tha God that while he was not very religious, he believed in God as he'd been raised in a heavy Christian background.

As a child, he showed an interest in poetry. He remembers a time in first grade when a teacher asked the class to make cards for Mother's Day and was surprised by what he came up with.

When he was six-years-old, Victor took him to his first concert at the Birmingham Civic Center. He would see Run-DMC, Whodini, the Beastie Boys, and LL Cool J on their Raising Hell tour of summer 1986. Two years later, he would also see Kool Moe Dee and Eric B perform, among a lineup of several other prominent rappers at the time. In 1989, he would see N.W.A perform, too.

He has mentioned that the walls of his childhood bedroom were covered up by his brother's posters.

His maternal grandfather's death prompted an unpleasant change in his mother's family that would go on for years. The unpleasantness was mostly made manifest in how Vicky and her sisters would argue. Their arguments often turned physical, drawing blood on several occasions in view of neighbors who watched on as the sisters fought on the lawn.

All of this contributed to his mother's dissatisfaction and an eventual decision to move from Alabama to Atlanta. Two attempts were made.

The first was with a boyfriend of hers who commuted between Bessemer and Atlanta for work. It was settled that they would live at his place and they were packed up and ready to go. When the day arrived, however, he was a no show and left them stranded.

Almost a whole year passed before another opportunity presented itself. This time, it came in the form of a truck driver who his mother met at church. The deal was that they would stay over at his place until Vicky got a job and settled down.

The Davis siblings felt dubious about this plan, and they were correct too with all things considered. Still, this time things went according to plan, and their move proceeded without a hitch.

ELLENWOOD

They arrived at Ellenwood, Georgia, in August 1989. It was a place that did not feel all that different from what a young Gucci Mane was used to, at least not at first. A few months into their stay at Ellenwood, the truck driver and his ex-wife reconciled, and she, along with their child, moved in with him.

His wife made things unbearable for the Davis's. She argued with Vicky and even went as far as pulling down all of the posters that Victor had brought with him from Bessemer and throwing them in the trash.

It soon became evident that they would not be able to live with the man and his family for much longer, which would've been okay if they had anywhere else to go. Eventually, Vicky would reach out to his paternal grandmother, who sent her son, Ralph, to retrieve them.

Before this, Ralph's visits to Bessemer had stopped when Vicky found out he had two other children. This, coupled with the fact that he was seldom present when Gucci was growing up, meant that he was estranged from his father, who he barely knew. They were practically strangers.

His father moved them out of Ellenwood and lodged them into the Knights Inn motel, located on the Eastside of Atlanta.

ATLANTA

The Knights Inn motel was located in Zone 6, an area with a very high crime rate. Prostitutes stood on every corner, and robberies were commonplace. Drugs were sold in the middle of traffic in broad daylight.

All of this and more were things Gucci found very hard to adapt to, but he did adjust. Over a decade later, he would allude to Zone 6 twice: in the title of his 10th and highest-charting 2011 EP, *The Return of Mr. Zone 6*, followed by a surprise EP released in 2015 titled *Views from Zone 6*—the latter being a play on words on the then-upcoming Drake album, *Views from the 6*.

Things at the Knights Inn motel were no different, and after a year, they moved.

Their new place was located in East Atlanta. Still, he and his brother remained in Cedar Grove Elementary and High, respectively, a school in Ellenwood they had been enrolled in when they still lived there. This was because Cedar Grove had a good football program; because Victor, who was good at the sport, stayed because of it, it meant that Gucci could too. However, with this final move came what he would later refer to as a "deep financial fear." Constantly, his mother complained of being behind on rent, and sometimes they would not be able to pay the light bills.

Neighbors were also being evicted because of their inability to pay rent. This was a phenomenon he had never come across in his time at Bessemer. It was a place where families had lived for generations; a good example being his own paternal great-grandfather, George Dudley Sr., who moved there in 1915.

It was at this point that he realized his father was a con artist.

After a two-year stint in the military, Ralph Dudley returned in 1976. He would briefly attend college before working at several power plants until he got in trouble with the law and ran away. Not long after he left Alabama, he ran into a man who taught him the ins and outs of what it meant to be a con artist in exchange for learning about the drug selling business. Gucci Mane would learn to observe people and use whatever information he gleaned to his advantage from his father.

But it did not matter. Ralph's profession' did not pay the bills due to a host of reasons. For one thing, being a con artist was no longer as lucrative as it used to be. For another, his father was an alcoholic and a gambler, so as soon as any money came into his hands, he blew it on his vices.

All of this led to a realization on Gucci Mane's part that he would have to find a way to get it independently if he wanted something. So he started with picking aluminum cans around the neighborhood with a boy a few years younger than he was and taking it to a store for a few cents each. That boy was Otis Williams Jr., better known by his stage name OJ Da Juiceman.

When he was in the seventh-grade, he began to help his older brother sell weed, and even right at the beginning, it was something that came easily to him.

Going to Cedar Grove Elementary, Gucci would compare himself to his peers and find that he was lacking, and so it wasn't long before things came to a head.

In eighth-grade, over the Christmas break of 1992, he told his mother that he would like certain things for the holidays. She informed him that she would not be able to provide these things for him as they were in a tight spot financially. He tried explaining, but she wouldn't listen. Instead, she decided to placate him with a fifty-dollar bill, which he used to purchase two fifty-dollar slabs of crack cocaine—and just like that, it went from being a hobby to becoming a full-fledged operation.

Because he was inexperienced, a friend of his walked him through the basics of the trade and even introduced him to a woman whose house doubled as a smoking parlor and brothel. He writes in his memoir that while initially he was repulsed by the environment, he soon became desensitized to it. He quickly acclimatized to the drug business—even becoming more inventive in how he went about the entire thing. With every smart business decision he made, his reputation grew.

By his freshman year at Ronald E. McNair High School, drug dealing had gone from being a disturbingly eerie extracurricular activity to becoming his go-to source of income. Through it all, his mother remained oblivious.

She was overworked and had no reason to suspect her son was dealing drugs. He got good grades, caused no trouble at school, and was well-liked among his peers. There was no reason to worry, but even when she eventually found out, he had prepared a ready excuse which led to her letting him off easy.

At fifteen, Gucci had been dealing drugs for a few years, but he had never indulged in it. He was deterred by the addicts he came into close contact with every day in his line of work. So, it wasn't until he met an older girl with who he'd eventually develop a sexual relationship with that he first smoked cannabis.

His first violent experience occurred in 1995 when a man stopped him on his bike. He pointed a .45 Desert Eagle handgun at his head and told him to hand over his stash and money.

Gucci Mane would surrender everything he had, save the four hundred dollars worth of crack he had clenched between his ass cheeks. The incident left him shaken up. After a brief consultation with Victor, who would soon go to start basic training for the U.S. Army, his brother would get him his first weapon from a pawnshop: a faulty .380 caliber handgun and a box of bullets.

Shortly after this, Ralph was taken away by the police on charges of domestic violence after hitting Vicky with a vacuum cleaner. His alcoholism was a crutch he leaned heavily on. By this point, he'd deteriorated to a level where regular hospital visits had become a thing.

After his arrest, Vicky and her two sons moved for the fourth time to a different apartment complex, Sun Valley. Initially, Gucci Mane found it difficult to get back into his business's flow. He would go out sometimes late at night after all the other old-timers had left to deal drugs. He was a stranger encroaching into already established territories. This situation was not only inconvenient but truly dangerous, as it had the potential to become life-threatening.

Lucky for Gucci Mane, OJ and his family moved into the same apartment building shortly after the Davis' did. To avoid the possibility of trouble, he and OJ would head out to the Texaco gas station—a place that both rappers would later refer to in several of their songs.

You could get anything from beer to weed at the Texaco, and people who did not want their relatives or neighbors to know of their drug habit could go there to get their fixes. Since the gas station was positioned on a busy five-way intersection, the two boys would act like they were waiting to catch a bus even as they dealt drugs.

It is important to note that none of these illicit activities were carried out with the blessing of the couple who ran the gas station. While at first, they tried to chase the boys away, eventually, they realized that nothing they said seemed to be having any effect.

The Texaco was also where serious fights, gang wars, and shootouts happened. Meaning that the incident of being robbed at gunpoint would not be the last time Radric Davis was confronted with a violent situation.

One major event would be the time OJ's best friend, Javon, got beat up by a local street gang who called themselves the East Shoals Boys sometime in the fall of 1997.

This resulted from an ongoing feud that began when Gucci slapped one of them, an athlete who'd splattered food all over him. The blowback of this would come in many forms: strangers walking through the hallways of his school looking for him and an almost violent altercation at a friend's graduation party, which he and his friends managed to narrowly escape, among many other things. Javon's beating only happened to be one of them.

Things came to a head when boys on either side of the quarrel clashed in a physical altercation that lasted for some time outside the McNair premises. Blows were exchanged, and the Sun Valley boys used chairs and other things within reach to ensure a victory for themselves, after which they fled.

The encounter effectively ended a feud that had lasted all through the summer and into the new school year.

In the spring of 1998, Radric Davis graduated from Robert McNair with a 3.0 GPA and a HOPE Scholarship to Georgia Perimeter College. Still, because of how well his drug operation was going and how much of his attention it commanded, he took a gap year. It wasn't until his mother gave him an ultimatum that he took action and tried to attend college. Even then, he showed no interest in getting a higher education. Instead, he used the eighteen hundred dollars he was given for textbooks to buy more drugs.

In his autobiography, he summarized his college experience of pulling into the school parking lot in a luxury vehicle and talking to the coeds while wearing expensive jewelry and shoes. He bragged to them that he could count on both hands the number of times he'd attended classes for the computer programming course he enrolled into.

He was kicked out of Georgia Perimeter after two semesters in April 2001. An undercover cop who had had his eyes on him found his stash, which amounted to about ninety bags of crack cocaine. When he was confronted at the Texaco, he fled, but it wasn't long before the police caught up to him, at which point he surrendered himself. This did not save him from getting beaten up by the police. They proceeded to throw him into their cruiser. Instead of taking him to the station for a mug shot, they took him to a hospital to treat his injuries. He was then taken to the DeKalb County Jail. When given a chance to make one call, he chose his mother, but this proved to be a mistake as their conversation ended with her essentially kicking him out of their home.

A few months later, Gucci was sentenced to ninety days in county jail. The judge warned him about having committed such a severe crime that could have him incarcerated for up to thirty years.

This came after he'd agreed to a plea deal and probationary period, which would allow his first felony to get struck off his record under Georgia's First Offenders Act (FOA). This act is a provision of Georgia law that allows people to enter a plea of guilty but avoid a criminal conviction. At the same time, he understood the judge's warning, he found that he was once again in a hard spot. He'd used all his savings to hire a lawyer to defend him. He also needed to get a new place to live since he was no longer welcome with his mother at Sun Valley.

Because he was, in all respect, still a student at Georgia

Perimeter, his lawyers convinced the judge to suspend his sentence

until the following school year was finished. However, it didn't take

long until he was back dealing drugs. He returned to familiar ground,

which was his old neighborhood and the Texaco. The judge's words

had made an impression on him, so Gucci continued to look for ways

to get out of his current lifestyle.

Naturally, he turned to music. Before their move to Atlanta,

his brother, Victor, was a huge music enthusiast. Victor went to the

Bessemer Flea Market to purchase any new album that had just

come out and play it on the boom box. This passion became

infectious, and the brothers would commit the lyrics to memory and

rap them to each other. Even when Victor was not around, Gucci

would diligently listen to the tapes on his own.

From a very young age, Gucci had already shown an interest

in rhyming, putting words together. He had begun rapping at 14, but since he loved the idea of it, this was not a thing he showed much interest in at first. He had an unpleasant vision of what rappers were like. What he found appealing was producing. This was mainly rooted in the fact that he was an avid fan of Master P, founder of No Limit Records' record label. Furthermore, he was inspired by CEOs, leaders, people like the late American rapper Eazy-E and Tony Draper, founder of *Suave House Records*. This record label exists to this day in Houston, Texas.

This was why he decided to take on as his first client, the fourteen-year-old brother of a friend who went by the moniker Lil' Buddy. This same friend later facilitated an introduction between Gucci and the then twenty-three-year-old beat maker Xavier Lamar Dotson, better known as the Grammy Award-winning record producer, Zaytoven.

They hit it off right from the start, and from him, Gucci was able to buy a batch of beats for one thousand dollars. He was ready to kick things off with Lil' Buddy. Before that could happen, he was mandated to report to DeKalb County to carry out his ninety-day sentence. He has mentioned that his decision to enter the music industry was also heavily influenced by this first arrest.

Seeing as it was his first offense, he only had to serve sixty-seven of the ninety days as he was designated a trustee. In there, he told his fellow inmates that he had his own record label, but by the time he returned from jail, his plans had fallen through. Lil' Buddy had given up his dream of being a rapper. Gucci was left with about a thousand dollars' worth of beats. It was Zaytoven who suggested that Gucci start rapping as he'd watched Gucci write Lil' Buddy's rap lyrics and teach him how to deliver them.

Initially, he was reluctant, but as time wore on, he began to warm up to the idea, and it wasn't long before his reservations began to fall away.

At the time, he'd been listening to the 1999 debut album of Memphis-raised rapper, Project Pat, and the content of this artiste's discography, along with others like C-Murder and BG, would give Gucci Mane a definitive idea of what it was he wanted his music to be like. The CEOs like Master P, who Gucci looked up to, lived lives of extravagance and opulence, subject matters he was not so well acquainted with, realities he did not exist in.

The goal was that his music would motivate others who were in the same situation as him without alienating himself from them. With this in mind, he and Zaytoven spent a lot of time together having fun and experimenting with their sound, finding ways to express themselves through music.

But when I think about trap music I think about those early days in Zay's basement. When I would go over early in the morning after a night spent juugin' in my neighborhood. When Zay would mix our songs and he didn't even know how to mix. The whole process was crude and unrefined. What we

were making wasn't radio-ready and definitely not destined

for the charts. When I think about trap I think about

something raw.

—From **The Autobiography of Gucci Mane** by Gucci Mane &

Neil Martinez-Belkin

GUCCI MANE: ON THE COME UP

GUCCI MANE LAFLARE & THE ZONE 6 CLIQUE

It was 2001, and with a decision to put together his first body of work firmly in place, it became a question of what his rap name would be. Growing up, he was used to being referred to as 'Gucci's son' or 'Lil' Gucci.' Hence, it felt natural to take on his father's nickname—which is how he went from being Radric Davis to Gucci Mane.

He bought more beats from Zaytoven and a producer called Albert Allen, who had once been the keyboardist for *Silk*, an R&B group formed in 1989 in Atlanta, best known for their number one Billboard chart-topping hit single, *'Freak Me.'* Because Albert knew more about the music industry than either Gucci or Zaytoven, he helped put together the collection of songs that would make up his first underground release, which he titled *Str8 Drop Records Presents: Gucci Mane LaFlare.*

Str8 Drop was a group he formed with a partner named Whoa. It was something more along the lines of a group of rappers than a record label, which his childhood friend, OJ, happened to be a part of.

Through an introduction set up by Albert, he found a place in Atlanta that helped print out CDs, postcards, and posters for *Gucci Mane LaFlare.* With these necessities out of the way, Gucci occupied himself with promoting his debut release by integrating the music into his drug operation, a package deal. He gave out CDs to friends and let them keep some of the proceeds of what they'd earned from selling them. Not long passed before he was almost out of stock. He followed up with what he has called one of the smartest decisions he made in his early music career: giving out the CDs' last copies to bootleggers. Gucci asked them to sell the copies, and in exchange, they could keep whatever profits they made from the sales. With this move, he'd ensured that his music would now be circulated all throughout Georgia and not just his neighborhood.

Gucci Mane was coming, and the world did not know what was about to hit it.

Shortly after this, he formed the Zone 6 Clique with another rapper, Red. They took pride in their independence, contented with the fact that rather than getting signed to record labels, it was money that came from drug dealing that they used to promote their projects. Despite the apparent success of *Gucci Mane LaFlare*, however, music was still not Gucci's first priority.

As it turns out, nearly everyone in the Zone 6 Clique was older than him. His drug operation appeared juvenile compared to these men, who moved several kilos of cocaine in statewide trips. But even beyond this, they were robbers who targeted drug dealers, taking away their stashes, along with amounts of money numbering in the six figures.

It wasn't long before Gucci began to do the same thing. He was only after money and drugs. He targeted people whose trust he had gained, breaking into their houses when they left their stashes at home and waiting to make them give it up when he didn't find it. When it became evident the type of person he was becoming, even his friends started to distance themselves. Still, it hardly mattered to him as his greed had now begun to overshadow everything. True to form, he began to expand his operation beyond East Atlanta, sometimes making trips to Alabama, where the demand for drugs was very high.

His arrival at Bessemer significantly brought about a shift in the family dynamics. It gave fertile ground for internal conflict to rise, mostly after a cousin of his, Suge, got arrested. The day before this happened, someone threw a firebomb into his house, so he had to move to a hotel where he was robbed, his drug stash was stolen. The authorities were called when Suge got into an altercation with the staff when he asked to see security footage.

When his family too began to pull away from him, he began to deal out of a friend's place in Birmingham. Here he met Bunny: the person who would introduce him to lean, a recreational drug beverage made from mixing prescription cough syrup and soda. This led the trap legend to develop a heavy psychological dependence on the lean combination.

Gucci's first experience with it was unpleasant, a mania that began days after drinking it that involved excessive paranoia, increasingly aggressive behavior, and impaired speech, among several other things. Only many years later would he connect the dots between that episode and the lean he'd drank before it began after a doctor told him the substance caused a chemical imbalance in his body.

He kept away from the beverage for a while, and not until he met a friend of Red's and the CEO of the Zone 6 Clique, Doo Dirty, did he start to grow addicted. Before getting introduced to Doo Dirty, Gucci had never sold pills. Not long after their meeting, he was not only selling them but taking them regularly too.

Despite their shortcomings, the Zone 6 Clique proved to be a very talented group of rappers. All focused on their music and very competitive during their studio sessions. Gucci found that he thrived in this environment and began to adopt a more disciplined approach to rapping.

Doo Dirty's involvement with the Zone 6 Clique, when summed up in its entirety, would look something like this: as a drug dealer, he wanted to make legal money in the music business, and because of this, no expenses were held back when it came to how lavishly he spent on the crew, from jewelry to letterman jackets, and then finally, Gucci's first-ever music video 'Misery Loves Company,' which cost thirty thousand dollars. Through Doo Dirty's financing, he could also afford his first-ever collaboration with a major artist, Juvenile.

Being his father's son, Gucci would go on to cheat Doo Dirty's nephew out of thirty thousand dollars in a drug deal, a move that put their relationship on hold for a couple of months—time spent keeping a low profile in Alabama, as the double-crossed nephew and his gang were making plans to kill him.

He returned to find that not only had all been forgiven, but Doo Dirty had paid off the bounty on his head as the offended parties had intended to shoot up his mother's house. Within minutes he was in Doo's truck, headed for a recording studio, where he met Shawty Redd, a producer he'd never worked with before.

This was where he would first hear of and speak to Young Jeezy: a rapper who, for any avid Gucci fan, cannot be mentioned without alarm bells going off. But all of this would happen subsequently, and over their first conversation, Jeezy let him know that he was a fan of his music, most especially 'Muscles in My Hand' off his *LaFlare* record.

BLACK TEE & SO ICY

In the fall of 2003, members of *Str8 Drop* would drop 'Black Tee,' a darker take on the *Dem Franchize Boyz* hit record 'White Tee.' Immediately, the song gained a massive following. Because he happened to have the first verse—where he had mentioned his name, DJs began to credit it as Gucci Mane's record when it started getting radio play.

It got his name out into Atlanta, and Gucci began to promote 'Black Tee' as his song when he started going to clubs and performing it. This caused a quarrel between him and members of Str8 Drop, which only escalated when they collided with the Zone 6

Clique at the Libra Ballroom, or Libra—a club where he'd built a following. This would lead Str8 Drop to rename themselves Neva Again, a pledge to never again deal with Gucci Mane. He was not present at the shooting of the 'Black Tee' music video, and a man with a bandana covering his face rapped his verse.

Gucci made a 'Black Tee' remix, and it was in the course of distributing the CDs that he met Coach K, the manager of Young Jeezy. He arrived with a proposal that Gucci and Jeezy collaborate, which he accepted.

Two days later, he and Jeezy were in the studio, but they couldn't bring themselves to agree on anything. Then Gucci asked to have Zaytoven brought into the studio. Zaytoven suggested the beat. After hearing the lyrics of the hook that Gucci had written, everyone was on board with that except Jeezy, who was eventually persuaded to record his part in what would be 'So Icy.'

Consequently, what came next was a promotion for 'So Icy' and the 'Black Tee' remix, which Young Jeezy had asked if he could hop on to. The songs were played in clubs at first. Still, it was only a matter of time before they received radio airplay. As a result, Gucci's reputation hit the ground running, and he began to get approached by record labels.

The first was T.I.'s *Grand Hustle*. Clay Evans, the vice president of the label, had taken an interest in Gucci's career from his open mic days at the Libra, going as far as booking him paid shows. He got introduced to T.I. and was offered a fifty-fifty partnership that would involve them footing the bills for the production cost, but what gave him pause was the fact that he was being offered no money upfront. Eventually, he turned down their offer.

After them, he met Jacob York, nicknamed the Chancellor for the role he'd played in brokering artists' careers like the Notorious

B.I.G. and Lil' Kim. Jacob flew him out to New York to meet the representatives of labels like *Universal*, *Atlantic*, and *Warner Bros*; like *Grand Hustle,* their offers left much to be desired. Eventually, he went back to Atlanta without a deal. However, it must be said that the trip hadn't been a complete waste as he returned with a sense of his worth in the industry.

The trip to New York had also left Jacob with some misgivings as to the capabilities of major labels to manage Gucci Mane, seeing as they lacked an understanding of the southern rap scene. Eventually, he set up a meeting with a local independent label named Big Cat Recordings. This label brought Khia, best known for her worldwide hit single, 'My Neck, My Back,' to prominence. Marlon 'Big Cat' Rowe offered not only a fifty-fifty partnership but also money to reimburse him for all he'd invested in his career up to that point. Finally, Gucci was getting what he wanted. With this on the table, he left the Zone 6 Clique, forming his own label *LaFlare Entertainment* as part of a joint venture with *Big Cat.*

Gucci was offered one hundred thousand dollars up front for the rights to 'So Icy' by Young Jeezy's record label, Def Jam, who wanted it for his debut album, *Let's Get It: Thug Motivation 101*. Before that, he'd received another offer, but turning down Def Jam's offer was a move that kicked into motion the start of his enmity with Jeezy.

Their joint performances of 'So Icy' in clubs stopped. Further attempts to hash out their differences proved futile until Jacob suggested they shoot a video for 'So Icy' and do a remix. But things went sideways, and what could've been an opportunity to extend the olive branch became an opportunity for further conflict. Jeezy and the people he hung around with dominated Atlanta's nightlife. Using his influence, he was able to blackball Gucci so hard that even DJs around Atlanta began to cut off 'So Icy' before his verse came up.

It was 2005, and having offended the powers that be, it appeared by all indications that Gucci Mane was finished. The fact that everyone thought him down for the count only lit a fire in him.

As a result of overhearing a conversation regarding being a one-hit-wonder, he changed the album's name from So Icy to Trap House. On May 9th, 2005, Young Jeezy released his controversial song, Stay Strapped, in which he placed a ten-thousand-dollar bounty on Gucci's four-thousand dollar 'So Icy' chain—one that extended to his person as well. For the second time in his life, there was a bounty on his head. Gucci clapped back with a hard-hitting diss track, 'Round 1', and what came next was a moment that would leave its indelible mark on the rapper, one that at once changed public perception of him. Some moments cleave your life into two parts: before and after.

What came next, for Gucci, was after.

I just want to let everyone know I'm not a murderer. I was upset. I was scared a little bit but I had to do what I had to do. You gotta be a man about it. I'm not a bad person. I have remorse for everything that happened.

—Gucci Mane on a Phone Conversation

TRAP HOUSE & MURDER CHARGES

On the evening of May 10th, 2005, Gucci was with a woman at her house in Decatur, Georgia, when a group of men burst in—interrupting their liaison. How it happened remains unclear, and it has been speculated that he was set up by the lady. Still, the fact remains that Gucci shot Henry Lee Clark III (or Pookie Loc) during the ensuing scuffle. Clark was a twenty-seven-year-old rapper from Macon whose corpse was later found behind a middle school not too far from where the shooting had occurred.

Gucci was in New York City, on set at BET's *Rap City,* when he found out about the murder charge. *Trap House* was set to come out in the following week, so when Jacob suggested that he turn himself into the police investigators, he agreed, driving straight to the DeKalb County Jail as soon as he arrived in Atlanta. Five days later, he walked out of DeKalb County Jail on a hundred-thousand-dollar cash bond, with his mind set on promoting *Trap House*, which was already out. He believed that Jeezy was the person behind the attack.

With the release of his album and newfound notoriety, the public opinion of Gucci changed once more.

Two months after turning himself in at DeKalb County, he was apprehended in front of a club in Miami. He was pulled into the back of a sedan without having his rights read to him. At first, he thought he was being kidnapped until they arrived at Miami's FBI headquarters. He was led to a room with walls covered with photos of seized drugs, weapons, and money.

There, two agents explained that they'd been made aware of death threats against him. They then proceeded to ask him about a drug operation he knew nothing of. He begged off with an excuse saying he needed to sleep. By the time he woke up, he was informed that there was a warrant out for him on an aggravated assault charge against a nightclub promoter.

Forty-eight hours later, he was transferred to Georgia. He describes the two-day bus ride—where he was handcuffed, with his ankles shackled in leg irons—as the worst discomfort he'd ever felt. He was only allowed to use the bathroom once over the two days, and because of that, his entire body cramped, and he could not sleep. Eventually, he arrived at Fulton County Jail, an overstrained and understaffed facility rife with weapons, gangs, and corruption. A little over a month into his stay at Fulton County, he was attacked on his way to visitation. This event would've ended in him beating his assailant to death if an older inmate hadn't intervened. He was immediately taken to solitary confinement—three rooms away from the courthouse killer and rapist, Brian Nichols.

His treatment at Fulton County's solitary confinement can be interpreted as a reflection of America's flawed prison system. He was allowed out of confinement only once every day, flanked on all sides by armed officers, shackled down with irons each time he left to shower. It was inhumane. He was put through it all for *defending himself after being attacked* on his way to visitation. He began to talk to himself, and the longer he spent locked up, the more thoughts of Young Jeezy consumed his mind.

Over three months passed before he was let out of solitary confinement. It happened after he called out to a warden, who explained that he'd stabbed his visitation buddy with a pen—which wasn't how things had gone. Video footage of the event served as evidence. Only after it was consulted did they let him back into general protective custody. Gucci says solitary had broken him down.

He noticed that little progress had been made on his cases and consulted with Jacob, who let him know that he'd taken an aggressive approach with the DA, which had brought things to a halt. But Gucci was not satisfied with a standstill. He fired his attorney, hiring a new team of lawyers, which proved to be a good decision. These professionals got the ball rolling in record time, settling the assault and murder charges.

In October 2005, he pled no contest to the aggravated assault case. He was given a six-month sentence and six and a half years' probation. Still, because he'd already spent three months at Fulton County, he was let out in January 2006.

Gucci's prison stint cost him over two hundred thousand dollars, and even though *Trap House* had sold over 150,000 dollars, he saw none of the profits. It seemed the numbers weren't adding up. Even beyond this, he'd given Big Cat a sum of money to hold onto for him before he went to jail, but each time he brought it up, it seemed like the latter always had an excuse. He smelt a rat.

Part of his plea deal included a specified amount of community service hours that he would have to fulfill. Giving back to the community was already something that Gucci Mane had been thinking about even before taking the plea. So, when Jacob asked him to meet up at Big Cat's office to introduce him to someone who'd help get his nonprofit idea going, he consented.

This is how he met Deborah Antney. She confirmed his suspicions that the stakeholders at Big Cat Records were not acting for his own benefit. Later that week, he would leave the set of the video shoot for 'Go Ahead'—a song that had blown up during his six-month sentence; effectively, putting an end to his business dealings with Big Cat and Jacob.

Finding himself at odds with his record label, Gucci returned to hanging out with the old Zone 6 crew, dealing drugs as if he had never left. As his track record in music hadn't been a success up to that point, he became apathetic to the music industry, a feeling that worsened after the release of 'My Chain,' the first single off *Hard to Kill*, which was set to be his sophomore release.

It would develop into a well-worn habit as the years progressed: him returning to dealing drugs whenever the response to his music was lukewarm as a sort of coping mechanism, but on this occasion, he was pulled out of his spiral through an intervention by his mom, Vicky, who he was surprised to see as mother and son had not been on good terms since she booted him out of the house in 2001 after his first run-in with the law.

Beside her stood Deborah Antney, who'd been trying to get a hold of him since the video shoot for 'Go Ahead' fell through. She told him that he was throwing his life away and asked why he would risk his chance to make it by falling into old habits. After both women left, Deborah's words took root and once more lit a fire in him. Gucci was back on track.

He became fast friends with a man called Shawty Lo, a member of the rap crew D4L who'd had their song 'Laffy Taffy' hit Number one on the Billboard charts the month he returned from prison. Shawty Lo had his own studio, and because they'd built up a fast friendship, he let Gucci know that he could record there free of charge. In return, Gucci helped with whatever it was Shawty needed, from cameos to music features, all without charge. Another person who would leave an impact on Gucci Mane's career was David Sweeten, professionally known as DJ Burn One, who had been a high schooler. It was he who introduced Gucci to the idea of mixtapes. Together they worked on his first mixtape, *Chicken Talk*, which Gucci has called a personal favorite of all his mixtapes, and a release more than any of his others that captured his state of mind during the time he was making it.

In *Chicken Talk,* he dissed every single Big Cat artist, and when at first Gucci tried to sell copies of it at a flea market, he was turned down. But as fate would have it, within minutes, the very same man who'd rejected him reconsidered after watching him sell copies to a small crowd formed as his new tape boomed out of Burn One's truck. The mixtape returned him to his rising star status. By this point, Deborah Antney had begun to manage his business affairs. She became like family to him and is Juaquin James Malphurs' mother, better known as the American rapper Waka Flocka Flame.

Through Deborah, he met Jimmy Henchman, the CEO of an artist management company at the time. The latter agreed to get him a new deal with a major label while helping him hash out a way to fulfill his obligations to *Big Cat*.

While this was going on, Big *Cat Records* went public with *Hard to Kill*—and two months after its release, Atlantic Records reached an agreement to buy out his contract with Big Cat.

He'd be an artist under Asylum Records, a subsidiary of Atlantic's president, Todd Moscowitz. In his earlier hunt for a New York-based record label signing, Todd had been the only person willing to go along with all of his demands. Still, the excitement shown by him had translated as red flags to Gucci, who at the time had been—and still was—deeply distrustful of monoliths in the music business. To combat the inevitability of this, perhaps, it was included in the agreement that he'd have his own imprint, *So Icey Entertainment*, which he and Deborah owned the entire percentage of sixty-six for him and thirty-three for her.

Not only had Gucci Mane taken the steps necessary in ensuring that he achieved greatness, but he was also willing to put in the work; but despite this, the murder of Pookie Loc was something he carried along with him. This incident had saddled him with a reputation he did not ask for. He was seen as a killer. In *The Autobiography of Gucci Mane,* he highlights two times he had his narrative get hijacked by others away from him to give a glimpse into how skewered public opinion of him seemed to be at that time.

He recalls getting a dinner invite from producer Scott Storch—who he was excited to work with, seeing as the latter had just produced Fat Joe's hit song 'Make It Rain'—and arriving at his ten-million-dollar mansion only to get introduced by Scott to his friends.

"This is the guy I was telling you about, the guy who everybody don't like." Before going on to add: *"You know, the one with the murder charge."*

Subtle attempts to steer Scott off-topic by an uncomfortable Gucci Mane proved futile. While eventually, he came to entertain the possibility that Scott had been on drugs at the time (this was at the peak of his career, a point at which his net worth was valued to be about $100 million—charging about a hundred thousand dollars for each beat he made—and later it came to light that he'd once blown $30 million on a six-month cocaine binge) he didn't know and left with a not so high opinion of the man.

The second was his fateful meeting with Rick Ross not long after the Storch incident, whose first words to him, he says, was: *"If I was you, every time I rapped I'd say 'I killed a nigga and got away with it.'"*

BACK TO THE TRAP HOUSE & FREAKY GURL

Gucci was beginning to gain national recognition and started work on his fourth album and major-label debut: *Back to the Trap*

House. However, the title would prove ironic as it ended up going in an entirely different direction from his 2005 release, *Trap House.*

It was planned that the lead single off *Back to the Trap House* would be 'Bird Flu.' Everything was set and ready to go but then 'Freaky Gurl,' a song off *Hard to Kill*, blew up. Produced by Cyber Sapp and sampling elements from a 2002 song titled 'Lick' by Joi, 'Freaky Gurl' was a song inspired by Gucci's white Hummer H2. It featured a hook which played on Rick James's 1981 classic, 'Superfreak.' It came as a shock to even Gucci when he heard it playing on the radio nearly two years after its release, as at the time he recorded it, he hadn't put much stock into the song. It would peak at numbers 12 on Hot Rap Tracks, 19 on Hot R & *R&B/Hip-Hop Songs*, and 62 on the *Billboard Hot 100* charts, respectively.

A tug-of-war between *Asylum* and *Big Cat Recordings* ensued over the publishing rights to 'Freaky Gurl,' further complicated by the fact that another of his songs owned by *Big Cat* named 'Pillz' had begun to pick up steam alongside it. When negotiations with his former label got nowhere, *Asylum* decided to take matters into their own hands by having Gucci rerecord both songs. Ludacris and Lil' Kim were added to the remix of 'Freaky Gurl,' and 'Pillz' became 'I Might Be,' where artistes the Game and Shawnna got featured.

He submitted two different albums to Asylum when they asked him to turn in *Back to the Trap House*: the first comprising of songs he'd recorded on a two-day visit to New York, done with the producers recommended to him as part of his deal with Jimmy Henchman's artist management company which stipulated that he would work with producers they set him up with for his major-label debut. It was commercial and had a lot of big-name features. The second included songs that are today considered his classics. Songs like 'Vette Pass By' and 'My Kitchen' that he'd made with Zaytoven and Shawty Redd.

But Asylum chose the first, claiming that the second album sounded like mixtapes and that they wouldn't leave much of an impact. He agreed, entirely ignoring his preference for the second version of the album.

Around this time, he began to hang out with OJ and Waka, who, at that point, was just nineteen-years-old. He saw Waka moving in a path that could only end in disaster and took him under his wings. Along with Waka's older brother Wooh, and their cousin, Frenchie, they formed the nucleus of young men. He started acting as a mentor of sorts too, who called themselves the *So Icey Boyz.* In fact, it got to a stage where he became so deeply connected to Deborah and her family that he lived with them. When he would eventually move out, the boys went with him, calling his new place the *So Icey Boys* clubhouse.

Of the group, he was closest to Waka, who he describes in his memoir as having a brother-like bond. It was in one of his studio sessions with producer Polow da Don while wrapping up his song 'I Know Why' (the fourth track on *Back to the Trap House*) that seeds which would germinate into Waka's profound career starting with his lead role in Gucci's label, Brick Squad.

"That dude who with you, Gucci," he told me. "I think he could be a star."

"You know what, Polow?" I said. "I been thought that."

—From **The Autobiography of Gucci Mane** by Gucci Mane & Neil Martinez-Belkin

To promote his upcoming album, it was decided that the remix for 'Freaky Gurl' would be followed by one for 'I Know Why'— but then about two weeks before *Back to the Trap House* was slated to be released, an artist featured on the remix died as a result of a sleep apnea disorder exacerbated by drinking lean. The artist was Pimp C.

For Gucci, his introduction to hard drugs came in increments. Still, it was lean that first landed him in the hospital, and it would be his go-to opioid as the years passed by so that by 2007, he'd come to develop a dependence on it. It was something he required to function, and without it, he felt a crippling anxiety every time the issue of radio interviews or live performances came up. A side effect was that he became constipated; still, unlike other rappers, he was on probation and had to be discreet in his usage of the beverage.

A weekend before the album was set to come out, he met Nicki Minaj at Columbus, Ohio, while opening for Lil Wayne on his Best Rapper Alive tour. Cited as one of the most influential female rap artists of all time today, with an estimated 100 million records sold worldwide under her belt—this was before the success of her breakthrough mixtape release, *Beam Me Up, Scotty*. At the time, she'd been a virtual unknown who began by saying she was a fan of 'Freaky Gurl.' He introduced her to Deborah Antney, who signed her to her management company Mizay Entertainment and later linked her up with a friend of his, DJ Holiday, who would host Beam Me Up, *Scotty*.

Back to the Trap House did not do as well as he and everyone else at *Asylum* thought it would, debuting at number 57 on *Billboard's Top 200* and selling fewer than thirty-two thousand copies in its first week. In Gucci's eyes, there was no one else to blame except himself for not going with his gut and insisting his label go with the second version he'd submitted. Pimp C's death's side effect was that *Asylum* stopped pushing 'I Know Why' as a single, and after that, Gucci's fourth studio project fell to the wayside. The fact that his latest album was a flop did not mean he had become irrelevant, however. 'Freaky Gurl' and 'Pillz' ensured he still got booked for shows all over America. He charged up to thirty thousand dollars a performance, which meant that he was not financially tight.

But a need to prove himself arose in Gucci after the disappointment of *Back to the Trap House*. So, he decided to flood the masses with music at every chance he got. He appeared on OJ da Juiceman's signature 'Make Tha Trap Say Aye' (a song that caused a rift between him and his childhood friend, though we will soon be getting to that) and began working on various mixtapes, scheduling one with every DJ he knew.

He worked hours on end in various studios as the plans he'd made meant he needed to record nonstop. This decision of his would change his entire approach to music, a relic of which we can still see today.

Prior to this new era, for example, he'd mostly written down his raps. But with the impossible schedule, he was on, Gucci delved deeper into playing around with freestyling—a process he'd started getting into over a mixtape of his, *No Pad No Pencil*. Over that time, he'd been shooting a documentary with Hood Affairs, a YouTube channel that today puts out new and unreleased footage of several R&B/Hip-Hop legends before they became famous.

Moving on to freestyles had not been a premeditated decision. Still, it was convenient and he delved into the artform wholeheartedly, easily recording as much as seven songs every day. Through this, he set a pace that few artists could ever match. Overflowing with ideas the way he was, and rapping into skeleton beats, so he would move on to the next project. And this paid off.

The man behind the legend continued to grow in prominence within the music industry, and the disappointment surrounding his commercial debut began to fade away.

Gucci's mixtapes were arriving with rapid-fire frequency, from *Mr. Perfect* with DJ Ace to *Definition of A G* with Memphis rapper Yo Gotti, produced by DJ Drama. All of this culminated in *The Movie,* with DJ Drama, which he describes as one of his most cohesive releases to date.

A recurrent observation from his 2017 memoir is that whenever things seemed to be going well for Gucci, he would always run into a stumbling block. True to form, a week before *The Movie* was set to come out, he went in front of a judge for a probation violation hearing. He'd gotten arrested over the summer when he was pulled over at a sobriety checkpoint, where he was charged with driving under the influence, possession of marijuana, and possession of a firearm by a convicted felon.

But this was not the reason for the revocation of his probation at that particular hearing. Rather, he was being charged with only completing twenty-five out of the required six hundred hours community service he'd had as a part of his plea agreement back in 2005.

It shocked Gucci, as he *had* been doing the community service, organizing a shoe drive, and heading out to schools with his probation officer, where he would address students, telling them to stay out of trouble. What happened was that his probation officer's supervisor did not approve of the community service he'd been doing, though he would've probably approved of him picking trash

off the streets, among a list of other humiliating things.

At the Fulton County courthouse, he had a year of his

probation revoked. His pleas, the backbreaking body of work he'd

spent the past year accumulating, all of it—for nothing. He was going

back to jail.

GUCCI MANE: UPS AND DOWNS

WASTED & FULTON COUNTY JAIL, pt. 2

When he returned to Fulton County for his second stint, Gucci signed a waiver to be in the general population. A state of events not at all similar to his last stay at the jail where being the public figure he was, his lawyers had arranged to have him put in a segregated part of the jail, as someone trying to make a name for themselves could target him. He has explained that the reason behind his choice was that at the time, it'd felt disingenuous to his person. As a rapper, he spoke of moving drugs and urban violence, so he felt that it would be hypocritical of him to hide away from the general populace in his time in jail.

At Fulton County, violence was rampant, a place characterized by the frequency of its daily fights and stabbings. In spite of this, Gucci faced no problems from any of the other inmates after the visitation incident of 2005 that'd led to him getting locked up in solitary for over three months. The residents of the jail largely respected him and, fuming as he was over the injustice of his situation, those who did not respect him knew to stay away from him and not cause any problems.

As a result, he spent most of his time there minding his business: smoking, writing raps, and keeping contact with the people outside by using a phone he'd managed to have smuggled in. Things went smoothly on his part, but the same could not be said beyond the perimeters of his incarceration. Trouble began with five words: 'Make tha Trap Say Aye.'

It was a song he'd made in Zaytoven's basement five months before being sentenced back to prison, which featured on his *So Icey Boy* mixtape, and it'd begun to get a lot of buzz, would've been welcome news if it was not being credited as OJ's song. Originally, he'd had the first verse; listening to it play on the radio, he found

that OJ had made it so that Gucci's verse was now sandwiched

between two of his, changing the whole dynamic of the song. And

now it was OJ da Juiceman featuring Gucci Mane.

'Make tha Trap Say Aye' would be so successful, it got OJ his

record deal at Asylum—a deal facilitated by Deborah Antney—and

Gucci felt happy for his childhood friend. After all, it was he who

introduced OJ to different markets, taking him on tour with him and

helping him build a fan base. But it must also be pointed out that he

felt double-crossed by a now signed OJ and Deborah.

On the one hand, he had grounds to feel cheated but on

another, it was a move completely reminiscent of what he'd pulled

during 'Black Tee' that it would've brought joy to any of the Neva

Again members if they knew of it.

As his release date neared, he and one of the DJs he'd kept in contact with over the course of his sentence, DJ Holiday—who produced the *EA Sportscenter* mixtape together—began to talk about making another tape as soon as he got out. Gucci wasn't keen on the name Holiday suggested, *Writing on the Wall,* but the DJ was adamant, and in the end, he acquiesced, guided on by the sentiment that he had wasted a lot of valuable time in prison.

'Make tha Trap Say Aye' had strained his relationship with OJ, Deborah, even Zaytoven; so, it was that things continued this way for a short time after his release until he freestyled 'First Day Out,' which reminded him to prioritize his relationship with Zay.

It was also around this time that he conceptualized the idea for what would go on to be his iconic song, 'Wasted.' He put it onto the *Writing on the Wall* mixtape and forgot about it. But the song had the same effect as 'Freaky Gurl.' With the potential he saw in 'Wasted,' he wanted it to be the lead single for his next album. The only problem was that he was not on good terms with *Atlantic,* and after the disappointment of *Back to the Trap House,* it appeared that they wanted hardly anything to do with him too. Beyond this, he had offended, T.I., the labels rainmaker.

Putting off the idea would've been a wiser idea, but Gucci understood that time was of the essence and approached Todd Moscowitz, who had been promoted from president and CEO of *Asylum* to executive vice president of *Warner Bros.,* a sister label of *Atlantic.* With Todd's help, he was able to move to Warner Bros., where from the get-go, he noticed that they were giving him the support he'd always wanted from a label.

His deal with *Asylum* had fallen through, the *So Icey Entertainment* imprint was dissolved, and he started a new one— *1017 Brick Squad,* named after his grandfather's house at 1017 First Avenue in Bessemer.

An implication of this was that Deborah no longer had the thirty-three percent stake in his label that she'd had in *So Icey*. This was not something that sat well with her, but Gucci was happy with the state of things, especially after the part she'd played in getting OJ signed. The fact that Waka signed to 1017 was also another thing that displeased her, but she recognized it as something outside her sphere of influence as her son's bond with Gucci had only strengthened over the years. Waka was so fiercely loyal to him that signing to any other label at that moment in time was not even a possibility.

By now, the buzz about him was at an all-time high; it could be mostly credited to how good 'Wasted' was doing. He'd been skeptical about collaborating with other musicians since everything that happened in 'So Icy,' but Gucci was hopped on a feature with Mario for 'Break Up,' which he calls a pivotal crossover moment in his career. He says that after that, he worked with a flood of big-name artists: Trey Songz, Omarion, and Jamie Foxx.

He recalls his first time of meeting Mariah Carey, who after he'd finished a verse that would end up on the remix of her 'Obsessed,' asked for his input on some of the other songs she had for her upcoming album, and off his cosign, OJ da Juiceman would end up on the remix of her song, 'H.A.T.E.U.'

With all of this happening, he decided he would call his sixth studio album *The State vs. Radric Davis*, and at this point, he reconnected with Coach K, Young Jeezy's former manager.

Gucci was slow to warm up to this old acquaintance considering the part he'd played in his rocky history with Jeezy, but he was able to put aside his reservations when the Coach booked him a number of high-paying features. Beyond this, he realized he would need the help of an expert as the stakes he faced in making *The State vs. Radric Davis* were higher than any other project he'd ever recorded.

Once more, his intuition proved correct as it was through him that Gucci met the Grammy Award-winning American DJ, Bangladesh, on one of his trips to Vegas—who would go on to produce his homerun hit, 'Lemonade.'

The State vs. Radric Davis was shaping up to be bigger than anything he'd previously worked on when, once again, misfortune came in the form of Gucci violating his probation by failing a drug test and leaving town without a permit.

To prevent a third jail sentence, especially at this very crucial point in time, his lawyers and Todd Moscowitz came up with a plan to check him into rehab, their reasoning being that the judge would not be able to pull him out of a facility into which he'd gone to seek treatment and send him to jail. This did not mean that he wouldn't have a court date set for a probation violation hearing when he got out, but the way they saw it, his chances of being let off with a lighter sentence than jail looked infinitely better on paper if he was just coming out of a ninety-day drug treatment program.

It was a good emergency response plan, but Gucci was resistant to the idea of not only having to spend money on a problem he did not think he had. He did not believe he was an addict, as images that came up whenever he thought of the word involved the broken-down addicts, he'd grown up serving in East Atlanta. Not only this, but spending ninety days idle, not *making* money, was an antithesis of everything he stood for.

Somehow, Todd convinced him into committing to the plan, taking it a step further by not only convincing the chairman and CEO of *Warner Bros.* to cut a check for two out of the three-month program but fielding the bill of the last month with his own money. They'd known each other since 2004, and a constant was that Todd had always fought for him, which was something Gucci liked about the other man. But with this last move, the dynamics of their relationship changed, solidifying into the ever-shifting but durable bonds of a friendship that would go on to last forever.

THE TALBOTT RECOVERY ADDICTION TREATMENT CENTER

Compared to the life he'd been living up to that point, Gucci found rehab boring. Gambling, women, $ 25,000-night hotel suites, and his insane work ethic meant that he was in need of constant stimulation, and the Talbott Recovery Addiction Treatment Center just wasn't cutting it. He describes it as an experience similar to that of Georgia Perimeter's—where he was physically present but not really *there*.

Still, he'd committed to seeing through the next three months sober, so that was a high point if ever there was any.

Despite his lawyer's quick-witted decision, the threat of getting thrown into jail by a judge when his ninety-day program ended was still a very feasible threat, and so, he realized that *The State vs. Radric Davis* would need to be prepared in case of that eventuality. With the help of one of the staff, he was able to sneak out of the center in the middle of the night to go and record. At this point, he stumbled on another interesting tidbit about himself: he was making some of his best music while sober. Gucci had always thought that to make music, he would need to be high, but he proved himself wrong, rising to the challenge by maintaining laser-focus on the goal at hand.

A big trend in the music industry then was live-streaming studio sessions, but the general public remained unaware of this state of events as he always made sure he informed whatever producer he happened to be working with at the time that he couldn't be on camera.

At around this point, he ran into Young Jeezy on a two-day break he'd been granted by the recovery center to reacquaint himself with friends and family. His old enemy had just dropped a new song in which he called out Gucci and OJ in response to a particular song off the successful *Writing on the Wall* mixtape. It'd been over four years since they last physically saw each other, and this was as a result of that over that time, several people had kept them separate. It was either they were never booked on the same night, or one of them would have to leave after a performance to avoid bumping into the other.

This particular run-in had been orchestrated by Jeezy who after taking a quick stroll with Coach K—as you recall, they had issues of their own, which was the only reason Gucci had agreed to work with him in the first place—engaged Gucci in a private conversation in which he tabled out the reason for this fated meeting. The tension that'd characterized all of their previous talks was no longer present, and the day after that, they met again and agreed to a truce, promising to even work on some new music together. They were ready to put their beef aside—an enmity that'd spread through the years, affecting lives outside theirs like oil through clear water. This decision, if successful, would unite the various factions that'd sprung up from each side through East Atlanta. And perhaps, even the beyond.

He was given another two-day break which he used to wrap up some loose strings on his album. Gucci was to fly out to Houston to record one of the only unfinished records, and in the middle of his flight, the plane he'd boarded struck turbulence, while in the hysteria that followed, he felt a sense of calm.

A year prior, he'd found out he had a son by serendipity alone, and even as he didn't know him well enough, Gucci was content by the fact that even if it were the end, he'd left enough to see that his son lived a comfortable life, setting out to achieve anything he wanted to achieve without taking the same risks that

Gucci took when he was younger. But Gucci lived through the experience and even managed to wrap up the song he'd initially gone out there to do. Still, the fact that he thought it was the end is a moment that has stayed with him to this day.

With a month left to go at Talbott, through persuasion, he was able to talk the staff into letting him head out temporarily ahead of schedule, to go to the 2009 BET Hip Hop Awards, where he'd been asked to perform three times that night. It was an opportunity he couldn't turn down as it involved doing songs with Wale and Soulja Boy, which would then devolve into his own set. He saw it as a culmination of years of hard work and misfortune finally paying off.

He hadn't been around to witness the success of *Trap House*, which was overshadowed by his murder charge; *Back to the Trap House* had ended up being a disappointment. Furthermore, he'd managed to hold up his end of the deal by staying sober through the ninety-day program. *The State vs. Radric Davis* was set to be released in the following month; his performances were received with an enthusiasm that surprised even him.

Gucci Mane was *the* moment. He'd just released a mixtape and planned to release three more in the following week. There was nobody doing it like him, and life was great.

But then he checked out of Talbott after completing the program, and the next day a judge sentenced him to another year in Fulton County Jail.

THE STATE VS. RADRIC DAVIS & GEORGIA'S MOST WANTED: THE APPEAL

Without missing a beat, Gucci relapsed as soon as he arrived in Fulton County, and he was livid. In his eyes, he saw this as an injustice, a deliberate choice to ignore everything he'd already sacrificed to *avoid* prison. This time, what he felt was worse than the reason that'd been given for the sentencing that'd led to his last stay at Fulton County, which was community service.

Some things began to fall apart almost immediately, an example being Jeezy who reneged on their truce by not recording a verse on Gucci's song like he'd promised and then making it out to seem like Gucci had taken it upon himself to remix his song after the latter recorded a verse and put it out. They would meet again after this particular stint at Fulton, a tension-ridden exchange that made evident the fact that things were back to how they'd always been, even though their earlier sit-down had made Gucci develop a reluctant sense of respect for his arch-nemesis.

Outside this, however, things were going right. Arriving after an outpour of mixtapes and independent releases, *The State vs. Radric Davis* was as successful as he'd envisioned it would be: a project in which he finally balanced out the demands that came with major-label albums while managing to remain authentically true to himself and his sound.

It sold 90,000 copies in its first week and debuted at number ten on the US *Billboard* 200, meeting with generally favorable reviews from music critics. And because his getting sentenced to jail had always been a possibility, the label had prepared for this by having him shoot music videos to seven of the songs on the album. He was wanted for his first solo cover shoot, and as these things went, he was finally breaking into the mainstream—to the extent that even EDM DJs who played in music festivals around the world were remixing his songs, and these remixes were taking off.

His protégé, Waka Flocka Flame, was also going from up-and-coming prospect to outright star, releasing mixtape after mixtape of records that kicked things off for him. Through a mix of hard work and sheer talent, Waka was becoming one of *1017*'s principal figures and all in his own right, too, without having to bank his widely-known association to Gucci Mane.

On the 12th of May 2010, Gucci was let out of Fulton County after serving six months of his one-year sentence. When the formalities were over and done with, he headed straight into the studio, where he began to record new songs, making plans to shoot music videos for a couple of songs which had taken off in his time away—which is how he met Keyshia Dior, then Keyshia Watson, and later, Keyshia Ka'oir *Davis*.

Jamaican-born and Miami-raised, she was someone he noticed from the get-go when he first saw her in Timbaland and Drake's 'Say Something' music video, and his attraction to her was instant. On the set of the video shoot, he did everything in his power to ensure she felt good and then asked her out to dinner later that evening. There, they spoke of her dream to launch a line of cosmetics with the money she'd saved off the sudden success of 'Say

Something,' and Gucci felt a kinship, saw in her a determination he recognized in himself.

Obviously, Gucci recognized something special in her, because as at the time of writing this, the actress and entrepreneur has a net worth that lies in the range of eight-figures. But let's not get ahead of ourselves and remain content with the fact that at the time, he asked her to join him on the road, caught up as he was in a chokehold of shows and studio sessions.

The State vs. Radric Davis would go on to be certified Gold by the Recording Industry Association of America for sales exceeding five hundred thousand copies, and everyone at *Warner Bros.,* including Gucci himself, believed that his next project would be even bigger. For his next album, he had the full backing of everyone at his label.

Following the success of his album, Gucci dove headfirst into a world of debauchery and expenses, blowing money harder than he ever had before on Ferraris and a three-hundred-thousand-dollar ice cream cone chain, among several other things. Life was a rollercoaster, and for a time, it continued on like this until 'Gucci Time' leaked.

It wasn't a record he'd considered in the running for the lead single of his upcoming project, *Georgia's Most Wanted: The Appeal*, but he liked it enough, and over two hundred thousand dollars had gone into the shooting of its music video. The leak would've been a slight inconvenience if 'Gucci Time' did not fall subject to the scathing reviews of critics, a reaction that threw Gucci off as he'd never expected that the single would receive such negative responses. He wasn't used to it. By this point, he was finished with *The Appeal,* but its release date was still a few months away, and promoting the project became one of the label's biggest priorities.

Quietly, at first, he began to spiral, withdrawing from the promotion process by refusing to show up at photoshoots and not interacting with fans. His relationship with Keyshia fell apart, and he returned to drinking lean after almost a year away from it. He retreated into himself, not able to deal with the backlash his single was getting. He had always been paranoid but turning to drugs to cope only worsened this quality, shoving him deeper into despair.

He and Waka were already having problems, and the main reason behind this was that he had fired Deborah as his manager after promoters who paid for a bunch of shows he missed never received their deposits back. It was, to Gucci, the final straw and ultimate proof that she couldn't continue to represent him in an official capacity. The move put her in a tough financial spot, as prior to this, she had already been fired by Nicki Minaj.

In *The Autobiography of Gucci Mane*, he recalls the 2010 MTV Video Music Awards red carpet moment, where seemingly out of the blue, he whipped out a stack of ten thousand dollar bills and threw it at the reporters, effectively making all hell break loose. According to him: by this point, he had grown increasingly erratic and emotionally volatile, and it did not help that before he was allowed in, ten LAPD officers showed up to discuss whether he should be let into the venue, which only increased his agitation. The flash of cameras going off as soon as he gained admittance only fueled his anger as it felt like they were mocking him and zonked out as he was; it felt natural to dip his hands into his pockets and throw money at them.

The Appeal sold 60,000 records in its first week, which was nowhere near expectations, and Gucci blamed himself for it, feeling that he'd failed them in spite of all the love and support they'd shown him.

His 2010 BET Hip Hop Awards performance of 'Gucci Time' contrasted the last time he'd been onstage in every sense of the word, where he'd been sober and feeling unstoppable. He felt like a shell of his former self, and to his eyes, there was a marked difference in how the crowd reacted to him this time.

After the awards, he went to Miami Beach, where he embarked on the kind of bender rock stars are famous for while holed up in his condo. He ignored the calls of everyone looking to check in on him mostly, and when he did answer, he'd cuss at them before hanging up. This went on for a week until intervention was called, which involved taking him back to Atlanta under false pretenses (for which he attacked his bodyguard when he realized the truth), where he was met by members of his inner circle at another rehabilitation center. Their pleas that he check himself in fell on deaf ears, and it wasn't until his lawyer warned him of a possibility that he would get thrown into jail once more that he finally let up, agreeing to a month-long stay. But even this did not last as he rationalized that this line of thought—checking himself into rehab only to come out and get sent straight to jail—hadn't worked before, and to his drug-addled mind, he decided he would not fall for it a second time and through the help of a friend, checked himself out after a week.

All of this would culminate in a showdown on November 2nd, 2010, at his mechanic's auto-body shop. Somehow, he'd managed to talk himself into a theory that the man, his friend, had cheated him out of some money, and when he got there, he began to scream at him. Authorities arrived on the scene shortly after him, and their entreaties that he calm down came upon him like water poured on stones, leaving no visible effects, save the fact that they made him more irate.

Only when his accusations got physical, with him beating his friend, did the police step in, blasting pepper spray into his eyes and wrestling him to the ground before handcuffing him. But Gucci was on a rampage and placed in the backseat of their cruiser; he stomped on the door of the car so hard that it got damaged. He was transported to a hospital for immediate treatments, after which he was once again taken to Fulton County, where he had his charges read out to him, a list that contained about seven offenses including but not limited to: running a red light or stop sign, driving on the wrong side of the road and damage to government property.

He was in a boatload of trouble now, what with having skipped rehab and the failed drug test, but even then, he knew things would go downhill when he was let out of lockup the next day after the prosecution dropped all of the charges leveled against him, as even they saw that the judge he was set to appear in front of the following month would have a long list of offenses to justify a jail sentence that he could cherry-pick from.

On December 27th, 2010, his attorneys filed a plea of mental incompetency, claiming that Gucci would not be able to intelligently participate in his probation revocation hearing—a move that he to this day approves of as, at the time, he said he'd lost his mind. But the judge on his case was not sold on their argument, as he'd twice in the past sentenced him to jail. This was put to the test when he was committed to a psychiatric hospital that discharged him after three days, refuting his lawyer's argument of mental incompetency.

But the whole ordeal had left Gucci at a crossroad, where he at once felt alienated and tired of having this reputation he hadn't asked for, and a few days later, he went into a tattoo parlor and walked out of it with the image of a lightning-struck ice-cream cone with the words 'BRRR' tattooed on his face—a symbol that is now synonymous with his brand, touching everything from fan art to tour merch.

It was a pivotal moment for him, marked by the release of an EP with producer Drumma Boy, *The Return of Mr. Zone 6*. It was at once a shift in his sound and a return to his values, and he poured into that EP all his anger and resentment, those feelings of alienation, everything resurfaced in his music. He took his usual fun and colorful approach to trap and turned it on its head so that on the other side, what came out turned notably darker.

In its first week, *The Return of Mr. Zone 6* sold twenty-two thousand copies despite its lack of promotion, and two weeks after its release, he would be slapped with a fifteen-thousand-dollar battery complaint. He posted bail but was held back for violating his probation in Fulton County, after which he was transferred to the Georgia Diagnostic and Classification Prison for three weeks, which he writes in his memoir as "three of the worst weeks I ever spent locked up."

There Gucci had his hair shaved, after which he showered and was transferred to solitary confinement. Eventually, he was transferred back to Fulton County jail, where he spent another month before he was freed. Summed up, this stint went on for about three months, relatively shorter than all of his other sentences minus his very first.

He came out to find that the rappers 2 Chainz and Future were making waves, and behind their big songs was Mike Will Made It, who he'd come to know over the recording process of his *No Pad No Pencil* mixtape. Formerly known as just Mike Will, Gucci writes in his memoir that the American producer's new pseudonym was a throwback to their first days of working together when he'd mentioned the phrase in a track of his, 'Star Status.' There had been bad blood between the two of them for a couple of years, but after this latest jail sentence, he and Gucci began to work together, so that three weeks following his release, there was a joint mixtape with Future; after that, a collaboration album that he and Waka had worked together on earlier that year.

In September 2011, he pleaded guilty to the battery complaint, and after the sixty-thousand dollar settlement, he was sentenced to another few months in DeKalb County again, along with probation of three extra years, and when he finally got out, he was shocked by the death of a friend which would've sent him into one of his spirals if he hadn't begun to work more with Mike Will, who he found took a different view from Zaytoven, his day one producer. But it was a good thing as Mike's influence pushed him to strive beyond the boundaries, he usually limited himself to, and this paid off when he released *Trap Back the Return of Mr. Zone 6*, which came out to largely positive reviews from music critics, some of whom said that Gucci was back in his element.

What came next after the relative success of *Trap Back* was Gucci's introduction to Hollywood—*Spring Breakers*, where he played beside other stars like James Franco and Ashley Benson— which would inspire him to start production on *The Spot*, one he also starred in. His foray into film proved to be an interlude; however, not long after, he released his *I'm Up* mixtape.

Once again, Gucci started making up for lost time. He was booked and busy, modeling for various brands, among which was the streetwear brand LRG, on whose set he spontaneously made the decision to shoot a music video for his song 'Fuck Da World.' He apologized to Todd Moscowitz, who he'd grown distant from after *The Appeal,* and it was he who came up with Gucci's Trap God moniker; a short while passed before he resigned and once more, Gucci was transferred back to his old label, *Atlantic*, which he had only bad memories of.

Like *Big Cat*, Gucci rationalized that he would no longer work with them by sorting out his contract, but it was a long process, and in the meantime, he was set on getting his career back into his hands.

THE BRICK FACTORY

Established in 1993 by former NFL player Bob Whitfield of the Atlanta Falcons, Patchwerk Recording Studios in Atlanta is a place that, on more than one occasion, set the scene for a momentous moment in Gucci Mane's life. Several of his hit songs were recorded there: the 'Black Tee 'remix,' So Icy' and 'Wasted,' to name a few. Years after their less than cordial first encounter, Gucci would meet Juvenile, the first major artist he'd ever collaborated with.

It was a place that held a joint sway over him, both creative and historical, with perhaps even a little bit of nostalgia thrown into the mix. He could always be found there whenever he was not out of state but following his decision to steer clear of *Atlantic,* a new alternative needed to be found as the studio charged expensively, and by this, it meant setting up his own studio, which he did.

Gucci called it the Brick Factory, named after one of his favorite studios to record at, Hit Factory in Miami. It was located in the heart of Atlanta and also happened to be where the friend of his who'd died before he released *Trap Back the Return of Mr. Zone 6* was shot and murdered. This gave him pause but eventually, he resolved to buy the property as the $150 per hour rates at Patchwerk would've drained a considerable amount of money from his finances.

He renovated and furnished the place, installing the three recording rooms with only the best equipment.

He did not know at the time that it would be a place where he'd serve as a mentor figure of sorts for the next wave of artists that were to come out of Atlanta while grooming their careers to heights even they did not know they were capable of reaching.

At the Brick Factory, he took on a more active role, checking into what everyone was working on and chipping in where he could. He had a vision that the recording studio would be, to quote him from his autobiography, "an incubator of talent." This stemmed mainly from the fact that most of the boys whom he'd taken under his wings were hardly ever around.

He'd been on the lookout for the talent he could sign to his imprint 1017 even before this, and with the arrival of Brick Factory, he began to sign rappers, up-and-coming rappers. The first was

Young Scooter, but then he would move on to Young Thug and eventually the trio Migos, whom Gucci and Zaytoven stumbled upon on YouTube. He describes his first meeting with Quavo and Takeoff (Offset had been in jail at the time), where he took two gold necklaces off his neck and gave one to each person upon noticing the fake jewelry they had on.

The Brick Factory became a place bursting with ambition and talent, reminiscent of Gucci's Zone 6 Clique days except with none of the robbery or drugs. When spring rolled around, he kicked it off with a trip to California, where the *Spring Breakers* premiere was being held. There he met Marilyn Manson, and at the movie premier's after-party, they got into a studio and made 'Fancy Bitch,' a song inspired by their first interaction.

Meanwhile, his relationship with Waka had deteriorated so thoroughly that its breaking point came when in his absence, the other man took files to a song that he and Gucci had made, which led to the events of March 15th, 2013, where he announced that Waka had been dropped out of *1017*, at which point they proceeded to throw jabs at each other on Twitter.

Days later, a fan claimed that Gucci had hit him on the head with a bottle of champagne while he was talking to a security guard about getting a photo with him and the Atlanta Police Department issued out a warrant for his arrest, to which Gucci turned himself in to Fulton County. A bond of seventy-five thousand dollars was set on the day of his hearing, and he posted it, only to get arrested the next day and transferred to DeKalb County for once again violating his probation.

By general consensus, it was believed that Gucci would never get out. Everyone assumed that the law must have had its fill of his misdemeanors, and it was now only a matter of making an example of him, which is why all the artists he'd spent time grooming at *1017 Brick Squad* tried to jump ship and save their careers which were only just taking off. But three weeks after his arrest, he was released and from DeKalb County Jail, and instead of trying to address any of them, he hopped right into putting in the finishing touches for *Trap House 3*, which to him was a culmination of his musical journey.

He was let out on the precondition that he would wear an ankle monitor and stay under house arrest as long as any trip he wanted to take was not work-related, and Gucci listed the Brick Factory as his place of residence so he would still be able to record. By all indications, this appeared to be the best and most practical solution for all the parties involved, but as time went on, it proved otherwise.

Gucci returned to find that the Brick Factory had become something more along the lines of a place to kill time rather than a place of business and creativity like it'd been before. Also, his old friends from the Zone 6 Clique were beginning to show up more often than he would've liked, and with them came problems that spilled into the vicinity of Gucci's sanctuary. His old engineer left,

which is how Sean Paine, an intern from Patchwerk, became the

head engineer at his studio.

GUCCI MANE: HITTING ROCK BOTTOM

TRAP HOUSE 3 & SEPTEMBER 13

Just like he'd expected it would, *Trap House 3* was received well, and even though its success flew nowhere near the radar of *The State vs. Radric Davis,* he saw profit as a result of the fact that he'd released it independently. People were starting to listen to his music again, and this was fulfilling.

But Gucci had a lot of legal issues to face, and this put a damper on the success of *Trap House 3,* which he found himself unable to enjoy. Adding to this was the cloud of tension that'd begun to hang over the Brick Factory and the artists he'd signed who had begun to defect from his camp.

He became paranoid, a side effect of how much stress he was under, worsened by the steady supply of lean and weed he drank and smoked on a daily basis—but his fears were not baseless: he was confined to the Brick Factory, a building in which a friend of his had died, that was located in his old neighborhood where he'd accumulated a lot of enemies in his time growing up. He'd faced many violent encounters by this point, and true to the first tattoo he got (an eye on the back of his neck to remind him to watch his back), Gucci's mind unraveled with every possibility he considered.

The fear made him anxious, and this resulted in insomnia so that he turned to the false comfort that lean and weed provided him more and more even if it was only temporary, such that his indulgences became, he writes, 'unsustainably expensive.' Gucci was spending over a thousand dollars a day on drugs. He was on his way to another full-on spiral; even though he recognized this, he could think of no way to stop it. Press pause and just breathe.

Around this time, the Brick Factory got broken into, and when a review of the surveillance footage showed him the culprits, he told them not to come around the studio anymore, which did not go down well with them, pushing him further into his spiral. Gucci describes his studio as more of an armory at around this point, with guns everywhere and a palpable feeling of unease that took on a physical presence felt by everyone as soon as they crossed the threshold into the building. Regulars stopped dropping by, and the mood turned even sourer.

All of this should've affected his creativity in some way, at least, but it did not, and he was still releasing new projects with eerie precision. In fact, a lot of songs recorded in his album *Diary of a Trap God* were done at about this period.

It was the sound of somebody at the end of the line, facing a decision: accept defeat or go down in a blaze. I was sure someone was going to kill me or that I was going to have to kill someone again. That wasn't a difficult decision for me to

make.

—From **The Autobiography of Gucci Mane** by Gucci Mane &
Neil Martinez-Belkin

He was dropped out of his record label for hurling insults at
its CEO and COO online, and this was only the beginning as he went
on an online rampage airing out grievances and even accusing his
former manager, Deborah, of stealing money from OJ da Juiceman
and French Montana. Over the course of the following days, it would
come to light that some artists who'd worked at *1017* were no longer
signed to them and also that the label might be dissolved as they'd
lost their distribution deal with Gucci's old label.

Only after his lawyer called him with a warning—calling his
attention to the fact that he was still in the middle of several pending
legal issues—did Gucci slow down and eventually stop. He tried to

pass it that his account had been hacked by Coach K for $5000; then the paranoia set in again, and he began to question his lawyer's motive, wondering if they were working for someone else. By his reasoning, attorneys came and went, and he was ready to let this one go for all he cared.

In fact, to prove his point, he drove over to his criminal lawyer's office, but he was interrupted by the arrival of authorities when he got into a quarrel with security. And even if he was let off eventually, the cops had found a loaded .45 next to his belongings which he'd denied though his fingerprints were on them. He felt his days were numbered and went into what he calls full meltdown mode. Several days earlier, he'd dissed major Hip-Hop artists in the industry, including Nicki Minaj, Drake, Polow, and T.I., to name a few.

This was self-destruction at its finest, most terrible, and as these things went, everything came crashing shortly after midnight on September 14th, 2013. *The Autobiography of Gucci Mane* begins with a prologue snapshot of the last few moments before and during his altercation with the police and eventual arrest. It starts with an admission that even though he'd had his pistol taken away by the police the day before, he still had weapons, and he was bracing for an imagined final standoff. The Brick Factory is empty, and everyone is scared of him. Keyshia has had enough, and this time it appears to be the last straw. Gucci surmises that if he is going to get thrown in jail, he'll serve his sentence knowing he handled the thieves who broke into the Brick Factory.

On his way there, he is stopped by a police officer, and with an already distorted idea of reality fueled by the presence of codeine and promethazine in his system, his perception of the situation turned warped, and he presumed they are would-be hitmen sent to get him or possibly kidnappers. When he is asked if he has any weapons, he agrees, warning them to call for backup, and as more officers arrive on the scene, he becomes more agitated until he is restrained and arrested for disorderly conduct. But even cuffed, he struggled until paramedics arrive on-site and subdue him with two tranquilizers, at which point he wondered if he was being poisoned before peacefully drifting off to sleep.

First, he was taken to Grady Hospital for psychiatric evaluation, but by the time he sobered up, he was in DeKalb County Jail. Gucci looked around the bare room he was in and realized he was on the mental health floor, on suicide watch.

He had a cash bond of a hundred-and-thirty thousand dollars, and he called Keyshia to come and get him out, which she promised to but ended up not doing. Later he found out she'd had every intention of getting him out but was unable to, as he had holds from a lot of his pending cases, something he had not known of.

At DeKalb County, Gucci experienced opioid withdrawal for the first time, and he describes it as an experience akin to his body craving for lean the way it craved for food. It was painful, but he carried himself through it by remembering Big Cat's words from 2005

to keep his head up. But he continued to purge, and over the next

few days, a nurse informed him that his frequent consumption of

lean over the years had slowed down his metabolism, making his

body retain all the weight—and that which he was now experiencing

was his body's way of getting rid of the excess.

September 22nd, 2013 saw Gucci going public on Twitter and

admitting that he'd authored all those scathing tweets, while for the

first time acknowledging his addiction to lean. He apologized to

artists like Birdman, Rick Ross, and Drake—who he'd dissed; asked

his fans to have him in their prayers; and lastly, he apologized to

Keyshia.

Two weeks after his arrest, he was sentenced to six months at

DeKalb County for violating his probation, and from there, he was

transferred to Fulton County Jail, whereas part of the intake

procedure, he was weighed and saw that in two and a half weeks

he'd lost twenty-five pounds. It was an epiphany that came before his decision to lose weight after receiving his sentence—the first of several small decisions that indicated a decision to take control of his life. He took up running across the stairs of the jail.

The DeKalb County violation probation sentence did not include any of the other new charges that'd cropped up with his latest arrest: carrying a concealed weapon, disorderly conduct for safety, etc., and on November 19th, 2013, he was indicted in federal court with two counts of being a felon in possession of a firearm. His case was picked up in the Violent Repeat Offender Program, and it was argued at court that Gucci was to get put behind bars. The stakes were raised higher than they'd ever been in Gucci's life, as the charges put against him meant that he was facing over thirty years this time.

He was transferred from DeKalb County to the Robert A. Deyton Detention Facility—a privately owned facility in Georgia that housed people awaiting the verdicts of their federal cases—and here he was reacquainted with Doo Dirty. Almost a decade had passed since the major ways he contributed to Gucci's career when he was on the come up, and even his personal life, but the old friends caught up, dredging up old memories and laughing for a night that would be the last time they ever talked. Doo had a bad reputation, and being associated with him could prove fatal, and so Gucci distanced himself.

Locked away, prerecorded tracks of his were released, and his reputation soared as all of the new artists he'd taken under at the Brick Factory began to come into their own light and making known to the public their respect for him. He writes in his memoir that while he helped in introducing them to the world, they helped him keep in touch with his fire, which in turn made him create music that would resonate with the times. A new generation of artists rose, people, he'd never had a hand in grooming, and yet they paid tributes to him in their music.

They kept his legend alive.

FEDERAL PRISON: GUANTANAMO NORTH & REBIRTH

Gucci Mane pleaded guilty to one count of retention of a firearm by an ex-convict on May 13th, 2014. It came as part of a plea bargain that stipulated he waive his rights to the loaded gun that'd been found in his lawyer's office. The plea deal also involved settling on a thirty-nine-month sentence instead of the thirty-five he'd formerly looked at. Later, he also pleaded guilty to the aggravated assault case of the fan whom he'd hit with a bottle, and he was given three years, though leeway was made to allow him to serve both of his sentences concurrently.

His lawyers requested that he be sent to a minimum-security prison that would offer residential drug and alcohol treatment programs, and while the judge was receptive to his idea, it did not fall within his jurisdiction to make such a decision. Eventually, he was transferred to a holdover facility, where he spent two weeks in solitary confinement. After, he was taken to the United States

Penitentiary in Indiana, a maximum-security prison, which housed

inmates whose sentences went across the spectrum, from life

imprisonment to the death sentence. Also known as Guantanamo

North.

It was a violent place, and his arrival caused an uproar; Gucci

maintained his dignity, keeping to himself and minding his own

business even though he was scared. He continued to exercise and

even took up reading to strengthen his mind, just like his workouts

were strengthening his body. He wrote raps in this time of reflection

and realized that he still had a whole lot to live for: his career,

Keyshia, his son. Gucci knew that something had to give before he

died of an overdose or gang spat. Things had to change, and he was

willing to put in the work. His stay in prison became a blessing in

disguise, allowing him the gift of perspective and time to come into

this new version of himself.

At first, Gucci's release date was listed as March 2017 since

credit hadn't been given to the time he already did before his sentencing. But in February 2016, this was corrected, and his release date got moved up to September 20, 2016. He'd released about twelve projects over the course of his incarceration, and it is estimated that in that time, he racked in not less than $1,300,000.

Outside, life was waiting for him—his family and a yet-to-be-made manifest comeback album with Atlantic, a deal that Todd had helped broker. He had an interview with *The New York Times* lined up and covered shoots for various magazines. There were modeling gigs and book deal offers. He looked forward to proving everyone who'd ever counted him out of the game wrong. He would have to make a stand, and he was ready.

Unlike a lot of guys in this place, I was getting another chance. My last one. I couldn't drop the ball again. I needed to do more than pray. I needed to make better decisions.

—From *The Autobiography of Gucci Mane* by Gucci Mane & Neil Martinez-Belkin

GUCCI MANE: LUCKIEST MAN ALIVE

EVERYBODY LOOKING

Gucci was released four months early from prison on May 26th, 2016, on the grounds that the time he had spent in custody (five months) awaiting his sentence had not been removed from his sentence. Something that should have been done. His release caused social media to explode, ardent fans of his making known their anticipation for new music, and he wasted no time, as, on the next day, he went ahead to put out his first single below the renewed agreement with Atlantic Records. It was titled, '1st Day Out Tha Feds,'—a sequel track to the cut-edge 'First Day Out,' which was released in 2009 at around the time he was beginning to have a problem with Deborah and OJ.

This sequel served the purpose of a manifesto, wherein he addressed things he'd done in the past, alluding to the time in 2001 when he was thrown out of the house by his mother after his first arrest. He addressed the disloyal friends, describing the pitfalls of prison life in succinct detail, and by the end of the song, it was clear to any who'd listened that he was finished with letting other people take control of his narrative to paint inaccurate pictures of who he was. In his two-year absence, he had gone from being just another rapper and evolved into an icon with a cult following, his impact so ingrained in the lives of youths across all spectrums of life.

He'd sobered up in prison and was so obviously changed that some of his fans struggled to keep up with this new image of him which sparked a short-lived conspiracy theory that stated he wasn't the real Gucci Mane but rather a copy of him created by the C.I.A., using his altered physical appearance and improved lifestyle as proof, but he denied it and taunted the theory on an Instagram post.

In May 2016, he started to post teasers of his upcoming clothing line, Delantic Clothing—the brand's name was taken from his full name, Radric Delantic Davis, and it was to feature a line of apparel that ranged from hoodies to sweatshirts and underwear. It would come out in June 2018, a collaboration with Todd Moscowitz, Austen Rosen, and Miss Info.

Next came his ninth studio album, *Everybody Looking,* and already known for his backbreaking work ethic; by this point, it would come as no surprise to find that the recording sessions for the album took place in about six days. He announced it on June 25th, 2016, and less than a month later, it came out, debuting at number two on the US *Billboard* 200 with over sixty-eight thousand album-equivalent units, forty-three thousand of which happened to have come from pure album sales. It would go on to become his highest-charting album.

Later in September, he linked up with the Rae Sremmurd—a Mississippi-born duo formed by two brothers that he'd met through Mike Will, who had his own record label that he'd signed them into in 2013. Gucci collaborated with them on their single: *Black Beatles.* It went ahead to skyrocket to be number one on the *Billboard Hot 100* and remained there for 7 non-consecutive weeks, becoming Gucci's very first single which was number-one as a featured artist. Through his career, he'd been—and is still characterized by his unpretentious attitude of giving artists who hardly anybody had ever heard of a shot and doing this on *Black Beatles* proved to be one in a long line of good career decisions he'd made, dating back to one of the first: letting bootleggers sell his last few CDs of *LaFlare* and keep whatever profits they made for themselves.

THE MANE EVENT

The year of his release may have turned out to be as busy as he'd anticipated, that with the release of several other mixtapes like

Woptober and a second album, *The Return of East Atlanta Santa*, which came out on December 16th, but things picked up a notch in 2017 when he married Keyshia Ka'oir.

Prior to this, he'd already released his memoir written in his time in prison, *The Autobiography of Gucci Mane*, which then went on to become a New York Times bestseller. Also, he'd released *Mr. Davis*, his eleventh studio album, which included his song *'I Get the Bag'* featuring Migos. It was another success as it ranked at number 11 on the chart, *Billboard Hot 100*, becoming his very own most accomplished single and marking yet another breakthrough over two decades into his already illustrious career.

His marriage to Keyshia had been a long time coming, seeing as she'd not only stayed by him through the worst of his ordeals—even making arrangements during his USP sentence that allowed him to work in the kitchen and eat better than the other inmates—but instrumental in Gucci's shift to a healthier, more balanced lifestyle, as he has stated multiple times in interviews. He'd made a habit of publicizing his dedication to her on Snapchat since his release, and he proposed to her after performing at an Atlanta Hawks basketball game.

The star-studded wedding is reported to have cost $1.7 million dollars featuring, among several other things, a $75,000 Swarovski crystal-encrusted wedding cake that Gucci cut with a sword, and was paid for by BET, which produced a ten-episode reality TV series dubbed *The Mane Event*, that showed efforts put into what some would dub the wedding of the year.

A fact that did not go unnoticed was the date of their wedding, October 17th or more recognizably: 10/17. Once again, Gucci proved he was capable of drawing parallels between his past and future by getting wed on a date with numbers that held much significance to him. He'd named his label *1017 Brick Squad* after the street number of his late grandfather; Walter Davis Sr. and he took this a step further by ensuring he said 'I do' to the love on his life on that date. And two years later, on December 23rd, 2020, Keyshia gave birth to their son, Ice Davis.

GUCCI COLLABORATION

Rumors of an official partnership between Gucci Mane and the eponymous luxury house began to surface in 2019 after he made a front-row appearance at the Italian label's Spring/Summer 2020 show with his wife. Seeing as he'd never hidden his appreciation for the brand, often wearing it head-to-toe, it was only a matter of time before collaboration came into the picture.

Before this, the brand had not attached itself with him, in any way, as a result of his public image and the controversies that surrounded him, but Gucci's apparent lifestyle change gave them a rethink and a week after he was spotted at the show, Gucci Mane said it out in the open that he would be the face of their

ComeAsYouAre_RSVP Gucci Cruise of the 2020 Campaign.

It was one of the moments that brought things full circle in

the rapper's life, seeing that his father had been so enamored with

the brand when he spent a few years of his service in Italy that he

became the *Gucci Man* and now his son who'd built something

unforgettable using that name was not only living up to the legacy

he'd set forward, instead, he'd gone above and beyond to

completely surpass expectations.

VERZUZ BATTLE

Verzuz is an American webcast series that was popularized

during the COVID-19 pandemic. It invites two artists, usually within

the R&B/Hip-Hop genre, to highlight their discographies. On

November 19th, 2020, Gucci Mane and Young Jeezy appeared

together on an episode for a face-off.

Their feud had gone on for an estimated fifteen years at this point, and several attempts to put it to rest over the previous years had fallen apart. But over the summer of 2020, Jeezy went on T.I.'s podcast, where he made known his desire to ease the strain between him and Gucci—whom he'd before then asked to do a Verzuz Battle, to which the latter denied; a case of their last attempt at a truce and how it'd gone down coming to mind.

Eventually, Gucci would agree, but when they appeared together at Atlanta's Magic City for most of the broadcast, the atmosphere was fraught with the familiar tension that'd characterized most of their interactions since 'So Icy.' As the rappers delved into the ten-song rounds that lasted over a three-hour session, subtle jabs were thrown, and Jeezy explained why he'd invited Gucci to take T.I.'s place in the face-off.

In the final round, they announced their plans to end their feud right there and followed this up with their first joint performance of 'So Icy' since 2005, when Gucci turned down Def Jam's proposal to buy his rights to the song. Their performance was followed by Gucci telling Jeezy it was all love and that he respected him for extending the olive branch; they both capped it off with an announcement that they would be going to a club together. They'd done what Gucci had hoped for back in 2009, putting an end to a feud that'd in many ways affected the city that'd shaped them.

Now that there was peace, there could be healing too.

GUCCI MANE: CONCLUSION

A man is more than the sum of all his parts and in no scenario is this more evident than the case of Radric Delantic Davis: A child so close to his grandfather he'd go on to name a business and marry on a date that reflected the numbers of the streets he'd grown up on. The baby of the family and its black sheep. An ex-drug dealer turned millionaire. An honor student who graduated with a scholarship from high school. A college dropout. A juvenile offender. A repeat offender. An addict. An ex-addict. A convict. An ex-convict. A friend. A boyfriend who was more trouble than he was worth. A husband, so madly in love with his wife, he told her not to spare any expenses at their wedding when she asked what budget she would be operating on. A brother. A troubled son. A father to two boys. An up-and-coming rapper. A pioneer of the trap music movement.

All of these are descriptors of the man he used to be and the man he is, and yet it is not as simple as capturing a person's life on paper in its completeness.

Gucci Mane grew up under conditions that others would fold under, and yet, he chose not to. Just like he chose to keep his head up as Big Cat advised when he was led away on the excruciating two-day bus ride and much later, as he was experiencing withdrawal in prison.

He'd been through so much, but through a combination of luck, skill, and hard work, he was able to become the man he is today—a man so far-flung out of his roots in the small town of Bessemer, Alabama, that he still holds close to himself. He did it, took control of his life, and spun the narrative around into one he actually controlled.

He took a stand, and so can you.

But you already know this.

References

1. The Autobiography of Gucci Mane by Gucci Mane with Neil Martinez-Belkin

2. Gucci Mane - Wikipedia

3. "The Autobiography of Gucci Mane" and the Struggle to Be Seen By Melvin Backman for The New Yorker (November 17, 2017)

4. The Autobiography of Gucci Mane Is the Story of the Luckiest Guy Alive By Rohan Nadkarni for GQ (September 19, 2017)

5. 12 things we learned from 'The Autobiography of Gucci Mane' By Kathy Iandoli for REVOLT (Sep 19, 2017)

6. Gucci Mane and Jeezy's VERZUZ Battle: Here's What Happened By Evan Minsker for Pitchfork (November 20, 2020)

7. Everything That Went Down at Gucci Mane & Keyshia Ka'oir's Wedding By Bianca Giulione for Highsnobiety

8. Growth with Gucci: A Conversation with Gucci Mane and Charlamagne Tha God (YouTube interview)

9. Keyshia Ka'oir Is All Love: How Keyshia met Gucci Mane, stuck by his side, and became America's sweetheart By Myles Tanzer for THE FADER

10. Gucci Mane Stars in Gucci Cruise Campaign, Announces Album By Sophie Caraan for HYPEBEAST (October 1, 2019)

Final Surprise Bonus

Final words from the author...

Hope you've enjoyed this biography of Gucci Mane.

It was an utmost privilege performing deep research and bringing forth these information to the public for you to enjoy.

I always like to overdeliver, so I'd like to give you one final bonus.

Do me a favor, if you enjoyed this book, please leave a review on Amazon.

It'll help get the word out so more people can find out more about our beloved superstar to support his legacy! (Plus, it'll help me a lot too. Thanks in advance!)

If you do, as a way of way of saying "thank you", I'll send you one of my most cherished collection report– Free:

Gucci Mane: The Complete Discography Collection From The Beginning to the Very End

A complete list of all of Gucci Mane's work that was ever published (or not published). As a Gucci Mane fan, you'll find this utmost valuable and cannot be missed!

Here's how to claim your free report:

1. Leave a review right away.

2. Send a screenshot to: jjvancebooks@gmail.com

3. Receive your free report –"**The Complete Discography Collection From The Beginning to the Very End**"–*immediately*!

Enjoyed This Book? Then Check Out...

Get to know the "Real" Curtis "50 Cent" Jackson - Behind the Curtains

Here's Just a Taste What You're About to Read in This Concise 50 Cent Biography:
Things most people might not know about Curtis "50 cent" Jackson

Origin of the name "50 cent"

By 1996, after Curtis was signed by RUN D.M.C, he adopted the name 50 Cent, a name which was inspired by a petty criminal by the name of Kelvin Martin, who used the same name. When asked why he chose the name, he said he chose it because it was a metaphor for change, which implied that he was going to do things his own way that was drastically different from the way others did. In his words, "the name says everything he wanted to say because he had the same 'go-getter' attitude as the original 50 Cent."

The 9 Bullet story

Most people know that 50 Cent was shot nine times, but there are parts that most people don't know about the incident. For instance, during the shooting, 50 Cent said he had a gun while he was being shot at, and while he tried to fire back, he discovered that the gun was not cocked.

Also, another thing most people might know is that the doctors who were operating on 50 Cent tried to carry out a tracheotomy, a procedure which involved them opening 50 Cent's wide pipe and which could potentially destroy his chances of ever rapping again.

His grandma, however, refused. She said, "If he couldn't do his music, he would be lost."

Kanye West

50 Cent was not an entertainer and an avid businessman, but he was also someone who knew how to do PR and capitalize on controversies.

One of the incidents where he exhibited the knack for turning controversies to his advantage was when in 2007, while promoting his third album '*Curtis*', he made an unprecedented move.
He announced publicly that if Kanye West sold more albums than his album (both albums were due to be released on the same date), he was going to quit music, and the fans bought into the challenge, thereby helping the both of them make good sales off their album.

When 50 Cent was asked in an interview about the results of the challenge and how he felt about Kanye emerging the winner, 'Kanye west gets the trophy, 50 gets the checks'.

Check it out here:

https://amzn.to/3eS9LOU

Or Scan the QR Code:

Printed in the USA
CPSIA information can be obtained
at www.ICGtesting.com
LVHW051208100524
779587LV00017B/1211